Crombie Jardine
PUBLISHING LIMITED
13 Nonsuch Walk, Cheam, Surrey, SM2 7LG

www.crombiejardine.com

This edition was first published by
Crombie Jardine Publishing Limited in 2006

ISBN 1-905102-51-8

Compiled by Gerd de Ley
Translations by David Potter

Designed by Stewart Ferris

Printed and bound in Great Britain by
William Clowes Ltd, Beccles, Suffolk

CONTENTS

A day without you
is like three years alone.
Chinese Proverb

I'll chase you until you catch me.
Marcel Achard

INTRODUCTION

Let's talk about love. It's the air that
we breathe, yet it takes our breath
away. It's all around, yet it's hard to find.
It's a sickness and the best medicine.
It's about giving and about taking. One
can fall into it and one can fall out of
it. It's free, but it can cost you dear.
Love knows no bounds, yet it binds.
Sometimes love is brief; sometimes
it lasts forever.

LET'S TALK ABOUT LOVE, BABY!

Let's Talk About Love, Baby captures a little of the love out there in the words of the famous and the not so famous. Anyone can fall in love after all. So if you're searching for the right way to tell someone how much you love them, or are hoping that someone you love is seeking the words to tell you, you'll be sure to find inspiration here.

Go talk!

Gerd de Ley

LOVE IS . . .

Love is the irresistible desire to be irresistibly desired.
Mark Twain

Love is the silent saying and saying of a single name.
Mignon McLaughlin

Love is friendship set to music.
E. Joseph Cossmann

LET'S TALK ABOUT LOVE, BABY!

Love is being stupid together.
Paul Valéry

Love is a great beautifier.
Louisa May Alcott

Love is a game that two can play and both win.
Eva Gabor

Maybe love is like luck. You have to go all the way to find it.
Robert Mitchum

Love is an electric blanket with somebody else in control of the switch.
Cathy Carlyle

Love is an act of endless forgiveness, a tender look which becomes a habit.
Peter Ustinov

Love is the master key that opens the gates of happiness.
Oliver Wendell Holmes

LET'S TALK ABOUT LOVE, BABY!

Love is one of the leading causes of life.
Ashleigh Brilliant

Love is when the other person's happiness is more important than your own.
H. Jackson Brown, Jr.

Love is, above all, the gift of oneself.
Jean Anouilh

Love is life. And if you miss love, you miss life.
Leo Buscaglia

LET'S TALK ABOUT LOVE, BABY!

Love is a feeling you feel when you're about to feel a feeling you never felt before.
Flip Wilson

Love doesn't make the world go 'round. Love is what makes the ride worthwhile.
Franklin P. Jones

Love is the greatest and the most irresistible force in the world, and our hope of heaven.
Barbara Cartland

LET'S TALK ABOUT LOVE, BABY!

Love is like dew that falls on both nettles and lilies.
Swedish Proverb

If I know what love is, it is because of you.
Herman Hesse

I may not be a smart man but I know what love is.
Forrest Gump

Phebe:
Good shepherd, tell this youth what 'tis
to love.

Silvius:
It is to be all made of sighs and tears;
It is to be all made of faith and service;
It is to be all made of fantasy,
All made of passion, and all made of
wishes;
All adoration, duty, and observance,
All humbleness, all patience, and
impatience,
All purity, all trial, all obedience.

William Shakespeare, *As You Like It*

Love is patient and kind; it is not jealous or conceited or proud; love is not ill-mannered or selfish or irritable; love does not keep a record of wrongs; love is not happy with evil, but is happy with the truth. Love never gives up; and its faith, hope, and patience never fail.

Corinthians 13: 4-8

LOOKING FOR LOVE

I'm looking for the perfect pillow — I think it's somewhere near yours.
Ashleigh Brilliant

The minute I heard my first love story I started looking for you, not knowing how blind that was. Lovers don't finally meet somewhere. They're in each other all along.
Jeraluddin Rumi

17

Find the person who will love you
because of your differences and not
in spite of them and you have found
a lover for life.
Leo Buscaglia

TELL HER YOU LOVE HER

If you love someone, you say it, right then, out loud.
Otherwise, the moment just passes you by . . .
Julia Roberts

I could have loved you once and even said it
But you went away,
When you came back it was too late
And love was a forgotten word.
Remember?
Marilyn Monroe

It is not only necessary to love. It is necessary
to say so.
French Proverb

KISS ME

I married the first man I ever kissed.
When I tell this to my children, they just
about throw up!
Barbara Bush

Your mouth is a scarlet flower
bursting with honey -
and I am a bee.
Paul B. Lowney

Kiss me. Kiss me as if it were the last time.
Casablanca

A man's kiss is his signature.
Mae West

Make me immortal with a kiss.
Christopher Marlowe

I wasn't kissing her, I was whispering
in her mouth.
Chico Marx

LET'S TALK ABOUT LOVE, BABY!

To waste his whole heart in one kiss
Upon her perfect lips.
Lord Alfred Tennyson

Teach not thy lip such scorn, for it was made
For kissing, lady, not for such contempt.
William Shakespeare

Kissing is like drinking salted water. You
drink, and your thirst increases.
Chinese Proverb

A kiss is a pleasant reminder that two heads are better than one.
Anon

Remember, kisses are sweeter than whine.
Anon

Any man who can drive safely while kissing a pretty girl is simply not giving the kiss the attention it deserves.
Albert Einstein

A TIME TO LOVE

There is a time for work. And a time for love. That leaves no other time.
Coco Chanel

Had we but World enough, and Time,
This coyness Lady were no crime.
We would sit down, and think which way
To walk, and pass our long Loves Day.
Andrew Marvell

LET'S TALK ABOUT LOVE, BABY!

Come, my Celia, let us prove,
While we can, the sports of love,
Time will not be ours for ever,
He, at length, our good will sever.
Ben Jonson

I wish we could be together forty-eight
hours a day.
Gerd de Ley

LOVE AT FIRST SIGHT

Did my heart love till now? Forswear it, sight!
For I ne'er saw true beauty till this night.
William Shakespeare

When I saw you I fell in love.
And you smiled because you knew.
Arrigo Boito

A man falls in love through his eyes, a
woman through her ears.
Woodrow Wyatt

LOVE'S CHEMISTRY

How on earth are you ever going to
explain in terms of chemistry and
physics so important a biological
phenomenon as first love?
Albert Einstein

If our love is only a chemical reaction,
let us look together for the formula.
Hildegard Knef

THE COLOUR OF LOVE

In our life there is a single colour, as on an artist's palette, which provides the meaning of life and art. It is the colour of love.

Marc Chagall

THE MUSIC OF LOVE

The voice which was my music —
speak to me!
Lord Byron

Love is the harmony of two souls
singing together.
Gregory J.P. Godeck

If music be the breakfast of love, kindly
do not disturb until lunch-time.
James Agee

I like your snoring more than an aria of Pavarotti.

Amanda Marteleur

A love song is just a caress set to music.

Sigmund Romberg

Love is like a violin. The music may stop now and then, but the strings remain forever.

Anonymous

THE FOOD OF LOVE

I love thee like pudding; if thou wert
pie I'd eat thee.
John Ray

If music be the food of love, play on.
William Shakespeare

If music be the food of love, let's have
a Beethoven butty.
John Lennon

Come live with me and be my love
And we'll defy the storms above.
We'll lack for food, we'll lack for gold,
No lack of tales when we're old.
Christopher Marlowe

I love you so that I could eat ye.
Samuel Wesley

The hunger for love is much more
difficult to remove than the hunger for
bread.
Mother Teresa

LET'S TALK ABOUT LOVE, BABY!

I know that somewhere in the Universe exists my perfect soulmate - but looking for her is much more difficult than just staying at home and ordering another pizza.
Alf Whit

Your words are my food, your breath my wine. You are everything to me.
Sarah Bernhardt

My life will be sour grapes and ashes without you.
Daisy Ashford

LOVE WILL FIND A WAY

Love will find a way through paths
where wolves fear to prey.
Lord Byron

The course of true love never did run
smooth.
William Shakespeare

THROUGH LOVE'S EYES

If I could be granted a wish, I'd shine in your
eye like a jewel.
Bette Midler

For she was beautiful - her beauty made
The bright world dim, and everything beside
Seemed like the fleeting image of a shade.
Percy Bysshe Shelley

Life has taught us that love does not consist of gazing at each other but of looking outward in the same direction.
Antoine de Saint-Exupéry

THINKING OF YOU

If I had a single flower for every time I think about you, I could walk forever in my garden.
Claudia Ghandi

If instead of a gem, or even a flower, we should cast the gift of a loving thought into the heart of a friend, that would be giving as the angels give.
George MacDonald

ALL FOR LOVE

All that you are, all that I owe to you,
justifies my love.
Marquis de Lafayette

Love is everything it's cracked up to
be. That's why people are so cynical
about it . . . It really is worth fighting
for, risking everything for. And the
trouble is, if you don't risk everything,
you risk even more.
Erica Jong

LET'S TALK ABOUT LOVE, BABY!

I am in love - and, my God, it is the greatest thing that can happen to a man. I tell you, find a woman you can fall in love with. Do it. Let yourself fall in love. If you have not done so already, you are wasting your life.
D. H. Lawrence

You are my love, my life . . . my world.
Michelle Lozada

Life began after I fell in love with you.
B. Hodge

LET'S TALK ABOUT LOVE, BABY!

You're nothing short of my everything.
Ralph Block

Thou wast all that to me, love,
For which my soul did pine:
A green isle in the sea, love,
A fountain and a shrine.
Edgar Allan Poe

SO YOU WANT TO BE LOVED

If you would be loved, love and be lovable.
Benjamin Franklin

When you really want to love you will find it waiting for you.
Oscar Wilde

No one has ever loved anyone the way everyone wants to be loved.
Mignon McLaughlin

LET'S TALK ABOUT LOVE, BABY!

I really want to love somebody. I do. I just don't know if it's possible forever and ever.
Jim Carrey

If you wish to be loved, show more of your faults than your virtues.
Edward Bulwer-Lytton

Unconditional love is given by dogs and sought by children. Adults get what they get.
Unknown

DREAMING OF YOU

Better never to have met you in my
dream than to wake and reach for
hands that are not there.
Otomo Yakamochi

If we will it, it is no dream.
Theodor Herzl

If I had never met him,
I would have dreamed him into being.
Anzia Yezierska

LET'S TALK ABOUT LOVE, BABY!

I love thee, I love thee,
'Tis all that I can say;
It is my vision in the night,
My dreaming in the day.
Thomas Hood

Love happens when dreams
become reality.
Lacey Berry

THE PAIN OF LOVE

To love is to suffer. To avoid suffering one must not love. But then one suffers from not loving. Therefore to love is to suffer, not to love is to suffer. To suffer is to suffer. To be happy is to love. To be happy then is to suffer. But suffering makes one unhappy. Therefore, to be unhappy one must love, or love to suffer, or suffer from too much happiness. I hope you're getting this down.
Woody Allen

One word frees us of all the weight and pain in life. That word is love.
Sophocles

The heart was made to be broken.
Oscar Wilde

God is closest to those with broken hearts.
Jewish saying

The heart is the only broken instrument that works.
T.E. Kalem

To love is to risk getting hurt. Not to risk loving is the greatest risk of all.
Anon

Thou art to me a delicious torment.
Ralph Waldo Emerson

I think men who have a pierced ear are better prepared for marriage. They've experienced pain and bought jewellery.
Rita Rudner

Love is the pain you feel when it isn't there anymore.
Fernand Auwera

NO NEED FOR WORDS

When you're comfortable with someone you love, the silence is the best.
Britney Spears

A foolish man tells a woman to stop talking, but a wise man tells her that her mouth is extremely beautiful when her lips are closed.
Anon

LET'S TALK ABOUT LOVE, BABY!

You really love each other when it isn't
necessary any more to say it.
Charles Cahier

A kiss is a lovely trick designed by
nature to stop speech when words
become superfluous.
Ingrid Bergman

BORN TO LOVE YOU

I believe that two people are connected at the heart, and it doesn't matter what you do, or who you are or where you live; there are no boundaries or barriers if two people are destined to be together.
Julia Roberts

When you lov'd me, and I lov'd you,
Then both of us were born anew.
Samuel Taylor Coleridge

BECAUSE OF YOU...

My feet shall run because of you.
My feet, dance because of you.
My heart shall beat because of you.
My eyes, see because of you.
My mind, thinks because of you.
And I shall love because of you.
Eskimo Love Song

THE GAME OF LOVE

Love is the only game in which two can play and both can lose.
Texas Bix Bender

The love game is never called off on account of darkness.
Tom Masson

Love means nothing in tennis, but it's everything in life.
Anon

THE LANGUAGE OF LOVE

There are no other words to say:
'I love you.'
All lovers know that.
Jan Walravens

The Language of Love is international.
Gerard Reve

LET'S TALK ABOUT LOVE, BABY!

Please forgive me for all the nice
things I never said to you.
Ashleigh Brilliant

If my mouth were a pen, my heart
would write in blood and my veins
would write the words 'I love you'.
Caroline Lebrun

If my mouth were a pen, my heart

When your eyes talk to me it is
because my heart is listening.
Michel Vaner

LET'S TALK ABOUT LOVE, BABY!

Love is the language our hearts use
to speak to one another. For you, my
dear, my heart sings.
Amanda R. Byrd

The first duty of love - is to listen.
Paul Tillich

The Eskimos had 52 names for snow
because it was important to them;
there ought to be as many for love.
Margaret Atwood

GIVE AND TAKE

I cannot give you my love.
I can only share it.
Glenn Ridless

Dear Woman,
I give you my love,
would you be so kind
as to give it back?
Gerd de Ley

LET'S TALK ABOUT LOVE, BABY!

My bounty is as boundless as the sea,
My love as deep; the more I give to thee,
The more I have, for both are infinite.
William Shakespeare

The only reward for love is the experience of loving.
John Le Carré

LET'S TALK ABOUT LOVE, BABY!

For all the gifts you give
Me, dear, each day you live,
Of thanks above
All thanks that could be spoken
Take not my song in token,
Take my love.
Algernon Charles Swinburne

LOVE IS BLIND

Love makes a man blind and clairvoyant
at the same time.
Ludovico Ariosto

If love is blind, why is lingerie so popular?
Anon

Love looks not with the eyes, but with the
mind,
And therefore is winged Cupid painted
blind.
William Shakespeare

The best and most beautiful things in this world cannot be seen or even heard, but must be felt with the heart.
Helen Keller

You come to love not by finding the perfect person, but by seeing an imperfect person perfectly.
Sam Keen

Many a man has fallen in love with a girl in a light so dim he would not have chosen a suit by it.
Maurice Chevalier

I LOVE YOU THIS MUCH

With you I should love to live, with you be ready to die.
Horace

How much would you love me, if you loved me as much as I love you.
Paul Léautaud

My love for you is the only way to survive and the only thing worth surviving for.
Jo Röpcke

LET'S TALK ABOUT LOVE, BABY!

How do I love thee? Let me count the ways.
I love thee to the depth and breadth and height
My soul can reach, when feeling out of sight
For the ends of Being and ideal Grace.
I love thee to the level of everyday's
Most quiet need, by sun and candle-light.
I love thee freely, as men strive for Right;
I love thee purely, as they turn from Praise.

LET'S TALK ABOUT LOVE, BABY!

I love thee with the passion put to use
In my old griefs, and with my childhood's faith.
I love thee with a love I seemed to lose
With my lost saints, I love thee with the breath,
Smiles, tears of all my life! and, if God choose,
I shall but love thee better after death.

Elizabeth Barrett Browning

TRUE LOVE

True love comes quietly, without banners or flashing lights. If you hear bells, get your ears checked.
Erich Segal

True love doesn't come to you it has to be inside you.
Julia Roberts

If only one could tell true love from false love as one can tell mushrooms from toadstools.
Katherine Mansfield

LOVE'S CURRENCY

Thy love is better than high birth to
me,
Richer than wealth, prouder than
garments' cost,
Of more delight than hawks or horses
be.
William Shakespeare

Who, being loved, is poor?
Oscar Wilde

In the arithmetic of love, one plus one equals everything, and two minus one equals nothing.
Mignon McLaughlin

Come live in my heart and pay no rent.
Samuel Lover

Man has bought brains, but all the millions in the world have failed to buy love.
Emma Goldman

I can live without money, but I cannot
live without love.
Judy Garland

If women didn't exist, all the money in
the world would have no meaning.
Aristotle Onassis

HOME IS WHERE THE HEART IS

Without love, the rich and poor live in the same house.
Anon

If you do not let love reside in the body it is homeless.
Martin Allwood

Where we love is home,
Home that our feet may leave,
But not our hearts.
Oliver Wendell Holmes

IT LOOKS LIKE LOVE

To see her is to love her,
And love but her for ever;
For nature made her what she is,
And never made another!
Robert Burns

How beautiful you are,
now that you love me.
Marlene Dietrich

PUT YOUR TRUST IN ME

Doubt thou the stars are fire,
Doubt that the sun doth move,
Doubt truth to be a liar,
But never doubt I love.
William Shakespeare

When a man talks of love, with caution
trust him;
But if he swears, he'll certainly deceive
thee.
Thomas Otway

The best proof of love is trust.
Joyce Brothers

Love many, trust few and always
paddle your own canoe.
American Proverb

LET US . . .

Let's be egotists together.
Marcel Achard

Let us be vulnerable in each other.
Mireille Cottenjé

Let me be the sun that dries your tears.
Marc Andries

A LOVE SO STRONG

Our love is greater than illusion, and as strong as death.
Alberto Casella

If you have the courage to love, you survive.
Maya Angelou

Being deeply loved by someone gives you strength,
While loving someone deeply gives you courage.
Lao Tzu

Sometimes love is stronger than a man's convictions.
Isaac Bashevis Singer

We're very well-suited. Strong people need to be with strong people.
Madonna on Guy Richie

My love for you's so strong
That no one could kill it - not even you.
Anna Akhmatova

YOU MAKE MY
NIGHT DAY

My night has become a sunny dawn
because of you.
Ibn Abbad

Each morning as I awaken you're the
reason I smile,
You're the reason I love.
Jerry Burton

LOVE'S MAXIMS

We do not judge the people we love.
Jean-Paul Sartre

He that would the daughter win,
Must with the mother first begin.
John Ray

It is impossible to love, and be wise.
Francis Bacon

Gravitation cannot be held responsible
for people falling in love.
Albert Einstein

What the world really needs is more
love and less paper work.
Henny Youngman

If love is to bring all the good of which
it is capable, it must be free, generous,
unrestrained and wholehearted.
Bertrand Russell

LET'S TALK ABOUT LOVE, BABY!

'Tis well to be merry and wise,
'Tis well to be honest and true;
'Tis well to be off with the old love,
Before you are on with the new.
R.C. Maturin

Your love has a broken wing if it cannot
fly across the sea.
Maltbie D. Babcock

At the touch of love, everyone
becomes a poet.
Plato

LET'S TALK ABOUT LOVE, BABY!

Love much. Earth has enough of bitter
in it.
Ella Wheeler Wilcox

❤

The only abnormality is the incapacity
to love.
Anaïs Nin

❤

Love conquers all.
Virgil

LOVE PROVERBIAL

Love lives in cottages as well as in courts.

Love locks no cupboards.

Love makes labour light.

Love makes the world go round.

LET'S TALK ABOUT LOVE, BABY!

Love one that does not love you, answer
one that does not call you, and you will run
a fruitless race.

Love others well, but love thyself the most;
give good for good, but not to thine own cost.

Love rules his kingdom without a sword.

Love tastes sweet, but only with bread.

Love teaches even asses to dance.

Love tells us many things that are not so.

Love thy neighbour,
but pull not down thy hedge.

Love will find a way.

Love's merchandise is jealousy
and broken faith.

LET'S TALK ABOUT LOVE, BABY!

Love's plant must be watered with tears,
and tended with care.

Love's quarrels oft in pleasing concord end.

Love, a cough, and smoke, are hard to hide.

Lovers think others are blind.

LOVE'S RIVALS

I'm eight years younger, three inches taller and I've got boobs!
Sophie Marceau on love rival Isabelle Adjani

I love Mickey Mouse more than any woman I have ever known.
Walt Disney

He that falls in love with himself will have no rivals.
John Donne

HOLDING ON TO LOVE

Before marriage, a girl has to make love to a man to hold him. After marriage, she has to hold him to make love to him.
Marilyn Monroe

Love doesn't just sit there, like a stone; it has to be made, like bread, remade all the time, made new.
Ursula K Le Guin

LET'S TALK ABOUT LOVE, BABY!

Love cannot endure indifference. It needs to be wanted. Like a lamp, it needs to be fed out of the oil of another's heart, or its flame burns low.
Henry Ward Beecher

TO LOVE AND LOSE

To love and win is the best thing. To love and lose, the next best.
William Makepeace Thackeray

Great love affairs start with Champagne and end with tisane.
Honoré de Balzac

If you leave me, can I come too?
Cynthia Heimel

LET'S TALK ABOUT LOVE, BABY!

Should you be a tear,
I would never cry again,
for fear of losing you.
Bart de Pauw

Love is never lost. If not reciprocated,
it will flow back and soften and purify
the heart.
Washington Irving

I hold it true, whate'er befall,
I feel it when I sorrow most;
'Tis better to have loved and lost,
Than never to have loved at all.
Lord Alfred Tennyson

TWO BECOME ONE

We are two souls with but a single thought,
Two hearts that beat as one.
Friedrich Halm

If ever two were one, then surely we.
If ever man were loved by wife, then thee.
Anne Bradstreet

I am your clay.
You are my clay.
In life we share a single quilt.
In death we will share one coffin.

Kuan Tao-Sheng
He felt now that he was not simply close to her, but that he did not know where he ended and she began.
Leo Tolstoy

We are two and have but one heart.
François Villon

Whatever our souls are made of, his and mine are the same.
Emily Brontë

LOVE AND LAUGHTER

Even a trace of your laughter lightens up the room.
Michael J. Weithorn

There isn't one day that goes by that he doesn't make me laugh really, really hard.
Sarah Jessica Parker on husband Matthew Broderick

We cannot really love anybody with whom we never laugh.
Agnes Repplier

Sexiness wears thin after a while and beauty fades, but to be married to a man who makes you laugh every day, ah, now that's a real treat.
Joanne Woodward

To laugh often and love much . . . to appreciate beauty, to find the best in others, to give one's self . . . this is to have succeeded.
Ralph Waldo Emerson

TOO MUCH OF A GOOD THING

. . . you love me so much, you want to put me in your pocket. And I should die there smothered.
D.H. Lawrence

Then must you speak
Of One that lov'd not wisely but too well.
William Shakespeare

Ideally, couples need three lives; one for him, one for her and one for them together.
Jacqueline Bisset

LOVE AND SEX

My mother said it was simple to keep a man: you must be a maid in the living room, a cook in the kitchen and a whore in the bedroom. I said I'd hire the other two and take care of the bedroom bit.
Jerry Hall

Love is only a dirty trick played on us to achieve continuation of the species.
W. Somerset Maugham

Sex is a momentary itch. Love never lets you go.
Anon

WITHOUT YOU IN MY LIFE...

If you didn't exist, I'd invent you.
You're the one that fills my emptiness.
Only in the shadow of your skin do I know myself.
Only with you in my shadow do I recognize myself.
If you should fade away, my roots would die.
Gerd de Ley

Escape Me?
Never -
Beloved!
Robert Browning

LET'S TALK ABOUT LOVE, BABY!

So well I love thee, as without thee I
Love nothing.
If I might chuse, I'd rather die
Than be one day debarde thy
company.
Michael Drayton

Every day without you is like a book
without pages.
Fouad Abahusain

LET'S TALK ABOUT LOVE, BABY!

Life without you is like a tree
Without blossom and fruit.
Kahlil Gibran

♥

You are air for me.
I can't live without you.
Kadé Bruin

♥

Morning without you is dwindled dawn.
Emily Dickinson

TILL DEATH US DO PART

I did but see you passing by
and yet I love you till I die.
Walter Raleigh

If you live to be a hundred, I want to
live to be a hundred minus one day
so I never have to live without you.
A.A. Milne

Love doesn't die unless you kill it.
Fiona Cooper

Grow old with me!
The best is yet to be.
Robert Browning

I believe that if I should die,
and you were to walk near my grave,
from the very depths of the earth
I would hear your footsteps.
Benito Perez Galdos

LOVE IMMORTAL

And I shall love thee still, my dear, till the
seas gang dry.
Robert Burns

I believe if I should die,
And you should kiss my eyelids where I lie
Cold, dead, and dumb to all the world
contains,
The folded orbs would open at thy breath,
And from its exile in the Isles of Death
Life would come gladly back along my
veins.
Mary Ashley Townsend

FINAL WORDS

Love one another and you will be
happy. It's as simple and as difficult
as that.
Michael Leunig

Let those love now, who never lov'd
before,
Let those who always lov'd, now love
the more.
Thomas Parnell

INDEX OF AUTHORS

A

LET'S TALK ABOUT LOVE, BABY!

Woody Allen (1935)
American film director, screenwriter, actor, stand up
comic, playwright, short story writer and musician; born
Allen Stewart Königsberg, 45

Martin Allwood (1916-1999)
Anglo-Swedish writer, 68

Marc Andries (1939)
Flemish novelist, 72

Maya Angelou (1928)
US poet and playwright, born Marguerite Johnson, 73

Jean Anouilh (1910-1987)
French playwright, 12

Ludovico Ariosto (1474-1533)
Italian poet, 59

Daisy Ashford (1881-1972)
English child author, 33

Margaret Atwood (1939)
Canadian novelist, 55

Fernand Auwera (1929)
Flemish novelist, 47

B

Maltbie D. Babcock (1858-1901)
US theologist, 78
Sir Francis Bacon (1561-1626)
British essayist and philosopher, 76
Honoré de Balzac (1799-1850)
French novelist, 87
Henry Ward Beecher (1813-1887)
American Congregationalist clergyman, reformer and author, 86
Texas Bix Bender (1949)
US epigrammist, 52
Ingrid Bergman (1915-1982)
Swedish actress, 49
Sarah Bernhardt (1844-1923)
French actress, 33
Lacey Berry
US publicist, 44

Jacqueline Bisset (1944)
British actress, 93

Ralph Block (1889-1974)
US writer and producer, 40

Arrigo Boito (1842-1918)
Italian composer and poet, 26

Anne Bradstreet (1612-1672)
British born-American poet, 89

Ashleigh Brilliant (1933)
British-American aphorist, 12, 17, 54

Emily Brontë (1818-1848)
British novelist, 90

Joyce Brothers (1925)
US psychologist, 71

H. Jackson Brown Jr. (1940)
US publicist, 12

Elizabeth Barrett Browning (1806-1861)
English poet, born Elizabeth Moulton, 63

Robert Browning (1812-1889)
English poet, 95, 99

Kadé Bruin (1915-1985)
Dutch aphorist, born K.C. de Bruijn, 97
Edward Bulwer-Lytton (1803-1873)
British playwright, 42
Robert Burns (1759-1796)
Scottish poet, 69, 100
Jerry Burton (1937)
US publicist, 75
Leo Buscaglia (1924-1998)
US educationalist, 12, 18
Barbara Bush (1925)
Wife of former US President George H.W. Bush, 20
Amanda R. Byrd (1916)
US publicist, 55
Lord Byron (1788-1824)
English poet, born George Gordon, 29, 34

C

Charles Cahier (1807-1882)
French poet, 49
Cathy Carlyle
US publicist, 11
Jim Carrey (1962)
US actor, 42
Barbara Cartland (1901-2000)
British novelist, 13
Alberto Casella (1891-1957)
US playwright, 73
Marc Chagall (1887 1985)
Russian-born French painter, 28
Coco Chanel (1883 - 1971)
French fashion designer,
born Gabrielle Bonheur Chanel, 24
Maurice Chevalier (1888-1972)
French actor, 60

Samuel Taylor Coleridge (1772-1834)
English poet. 50
Fiona Cooper (1955)
British novelist. 98
Mireille Cottenjé (1933-2006)
Flemish novelist. 72

D

Emily Dickinson (1830-1886)
US poet. 97
Marlène Dietrich (1901-1992)
German-American actress and singer, born Maria von
Losch. 69
Walt Disney (1901-1966)
US film producer, director, screenwriter and animator;
born Walter Elias Disney. 84
John Donne (1572-1631)
English poet. 84

Michael Drayton (1563-1631)
English poet, 96

E

Albert Einstein (1879-1955)
Theoretical physicist and widely regarded as the greatest
scientist of the 20th century, 23, 27, 77
Ralph Waldo Emerson (1803-1882)
US author, poet and philosopher, 47, 92

F

Bejamin Franklin (1706-1790)
Prominent Founder, political figure and statesmen of
the United States, 41

G

Eva Gabor (1921-1995)
Hungarian-American actress, 10

Benito Perez Galdos (1843-1920)
Spanish writer, 99

Judy Garland (1922-1969)
American actress, 67

Claudia Ghandi
Indian publicist, 37

Kahlil Gibran (1883-1931)
Syrian poet, 97

Gregory J.P. Godeck
US writer, 29

Emma Goldman (1869-1940)
Lithuanian-born anarchist and feminist, 66

Forrest Gump
Character in novel of the same name by US novelist
Winston Groom, 14

H

Jerry Hall (1956)
American model and actress, 94
Friedrich Halm (1806-1871)
Austrian playwright, born Eligius Franz Joseph Münch-Bellinghause, 89
Cynthia Heimel (1947)
US humorist, 87
Theodor Herzl (1860-1904)
Hungarian-Zionist leader, 43
Herman Hesse (1877-1962)
German novelist, 14
B. Hodge (1931)
US crickete, 39
Oliver Wendell Holmes (1809-1894)
US poet, 68
Thomas Hood (1799-1845)
English poet, 44

Horace (65-8 B.C.)
Roman poet. 61

I

Washington Irving (1783-1859)
American author. 88

J

Franklin P. Jones (1887-1929)
US lawyer. 13
Erica Jong (1942)
American author and educator. 38
Ben Jonson (1572-1637)
English playwright. 25

K

Helen Keller (1880-1968)
Deafblind American author, activist and lecturer, 60
Hildegard Knef (1925-2002)
German actress and singer, 27

L

Marquis de Lafayette (1757-1834)
French aristocrat, born Gilbert du Motier, 38
D.H. Lawrence (1885-1930)
British novelist and poet, 39, 93
Paul Léautaud (1872-1956)
French writer, born Maurice Boissard, 61
Caroline Lebrun
French poet, 54
John Le Carré (1931)
British novelist, born David John Cornwell, 57

Ursula Kroeber Le Guin (1929)
American author, 85
John Lennon (1940-1980)
British singer-songwriter, 31
Michael Leunig (1945)
Cartoonist, 101
Gerd de Ley (1944)
Flemish actor and writer, 25, 56, 95
Samuel Lover (1797-1868)
Irish novelist, artist, songwriter and musician, 66
Paul B. Lowney (1922)
US humorist, 20
Michelle Lozada
US publicist, 39

M

George MacDonald (1824-1905)
Scottish author, poet, and Christian minister, 37

LET'S TALK ABOUT LOVE, BABY!

Madonna (1958)
American pop singer, born Madonna Ciccone, 74
Katherine Mansfield (1888-1923)
New Zealand-born author; born Kathleen Mansfield
Beauchamp, 64
Sophie Marceau (1966)
French actress, 84
Christopher Marlowe (1564-1593)
English playwright, 21, 32
Amanda Marteleur (1945)
Flemish aphorist, 30
Andrew Marvell (1621-1678)
English poet, 24
Chico Marx (1887-1961)
Pianist and performer; born Leonard Marx, 21
Tom Masson (1866-1934)
US humorist, 52
R.C. Maturin (1780-1924)
Irish playwright, 78

Mignon McLaughlin (1913-1983)
US journalist and author, 9, 41, 66
Bette Midler (1945)
US actress and singer, 35
A.A.Milne (1882-1956).
British author, playwright and poet, 98
Robert Mitchum (1917-1997)
American film actor and singer, 11
Marilyn Monroe (1926-1962)
US actress born Norma Jeane Mortenson, 19, 85

N

Anaïs Nin (1903-1977)
French-American novelist and diarist, 79

O

Aristotle Onassis (1900-1975)
Greek shipping magnate, 67
Thomas Otway (1652-1685)
English Restoration dramatist, 70

P

Sarah Jessica Parker (1965)
US actress, 91
Thomas Parnell (1679-1718)
Dublin-born poet, 101
Bart de Pauw (1968)
Flemish actor, 88
Plato (427 BC-347 BC)
Greek philosopher, 78
Edgar Allan Poe (1809-1849)
US poet and novelist, 40

R

Walter Raleigh (1554-1618)
English poet and explorer, 98
John Ray (1627-1705)
English physicist, 31, 76
Agnes Repplier (1858-1950)
Amerikaans essayist, 91
Gerard Reve (1923)
Dutch novelist, 53
Glenn Ridless (1963)
US aphorist, 56
Julia Roberts (1967)
US actress, 19, 50, 64
Sigmund Romberg (1887-1951)
Jewish composer, 30
Jo Röpcke (1928)
Flemish televison producer, 61
Rita Rudner (1956)
US Comedian and writer, 47

Jelaluddin Rumi (1207-1273)
Persian poet, 17
Bertrand Russell (1872-1970)
Logician, philosopher and mathematician, 77

S

Antoine de Saint-Exupéry (1900-1944)
French aviator and writer, 36
Jean-Paul Sartre (1905-1980)
French existentialist philosopher, dramatist, novelist and critic, 76
Erich Segal (1937)
US author, 64
William Shakespeare (1564-1616)
English playwright, 15, 22, 26, 31, 34, 57, 59, 65, 70, 93
Percy Bysshe Shelley (1792-1822)
English poet, 35

LET'S TALK ABOUT LOVE, BABY!

Mother Teresa (1910-1997)
Albanian Catholic nun who founded the Missionaries of
Charity in India; born Agnes Gonxha Bojaxhiu, 32
William Makepeace Thackeray (1811-1863)
English novelist, 87
Paul Tillich (1886-1965)
German-American theologian, 55
Count Lev Nikolayevich Tolstoy (1828-1910)
Russian novelist and social reformer, 90
Mary Ashley Townsend (1832-1901)
US poet, 100
Mark Twain (1835-1910)
American novelist, 9
Lao Tzu (6th century B.C.)
Chinese philosopher, 73

U

Sir Peter Ustinov (1921-2004)
British-born actor, writer, dramatist and raconteur; born
Peter Alexander von Ustinow, 11

V

Paul Valéry (1871-1945)
French author and poet, 10
Michel Vaner (1951)
French photographer, 54
François Villon (1431-c.1463)
French poet, born François des Loges de Montcorbier,
90
Virgil (70 BC-19 BC)
Latin poet; Publius Vergilius Maro, 79

W

Jan Walravens (1920-1965)
Flemish essayist, 53
Michael J. Weithorn (1956)
US scriptwriter, 91
Samuel Wesley (1662-1735)
English poet, 32
Mae West (1892/3-1980)
American actress, playwright, and sex symbol, 21
Alf Whit (1983)
US humorist, 33
Ella Wheeler Wilcox (1850-1919)
US poet, 79
Oscar Wilde (1854-1900)
Anglo-Irish playwright, novelist, poet, and short story writer; born Oscar Fingal O'Flahertie Wills Wilde, 41, 46, 65
Flip Wilson (1933-1998)
US comedian, 13

Joanne Woodward (1930)
Oscar winning American actress. 92
Woodrow Lyle Wyatt, Baron Wyatt of Weeford (1918-1997)
British Labour politician, author, journalist and
broadcaster. 26

Y

Anzia Yezierska (1881-1970)
Polish-born, American author. 43
Otomo Yakamochi (718-785)
Japanese poet. 43
Henny Youngman (1906-1998)
US Comedian. 77

101 REVENGE TRICKS

A LITTLE BOOK OF GETTING YOUR OWN BACK

CHRIS PILBEAM

1-905102-59-3, £2.99

1-905102-50-X, £2.99

1-905102-68-2, £2.99

If you have enjoyed this book,
please see others like it on
www.crombiejardine.com

All Crombie Jardine books are available from High
Street bookshops, Amazon or Bookpost
(P.O. Box 29, Douglas, Isle of Man, IM99 1BQ.
Tel: 01624 677237, Fax: 01624 670923,
Email: bookshop@enterprise.net.
Postage and packing free within the UK).